52 *Everyday Practices* to Strengthen Children's Emotional, Physical, and Mental Well-Being

H Is for Healing

Card Deck

Zahabiyah Yamasaki, MEd, RYT

Illustrated by Evelyn Rosario Andry

About This Deck

H Is for Healing is a soothing and powerful social-emotional learning card deck that provides children with the language for mindfulness, self-compassion, and empowerment. Crafted from a trauma- and nervous system–informed perspective, the cards correspond to the alphabet and introduce children to affirmations and activities they can integrate throughout the day to find a sense of grounding, calm, empowerment, and connection.

My hope is that these cards not only help children regulate their nervous systems in their ever-busy lives but also help them connect to their delight, joy, and wonder. May they know that they are enough, they are loved, and they belong.

How to Use This Deck

There is no right or wrong way to use this deck. Invite children to explore the cards and to choose how they would like to engage with the practices. They might be excited about a particular letter of the alphabet, be curious about a specific word they see, or be drawn to certain illustrations. Follow their lead, remembering that children are our greatest teachers.

As you move through this deck, I hope it also reminds you that tending to your own nervous system is one of the most powerful tools you can model and mirror for the children for whom you hold space.

Window of Tolerance for a Child

The "window of tolerance" is a concept developed by Dr. Daniel Siegel that explains how our bodies react to stress. This child-friendly visual, which was created by Christine Mark-Griffin, author of the *EMDR Workbook for Kids*, can help children notice when they're feeling out of control, in the zone, or shut down. You might even create your own visual with a turtle stuffed animal to help your child understand their nervous system. Start to take note of how the practices in this deck may help them honor their feelings, just as they are, and support them with tools that center their well-being.

Sources: Siegel, D. J. (1999). *The developing mind: Toward a neurobiology of interpersonal experience*. Guilford Press; Mark-Griffin, C. (2023). *EMDR Workbook for Kids*. PESI Publishing.

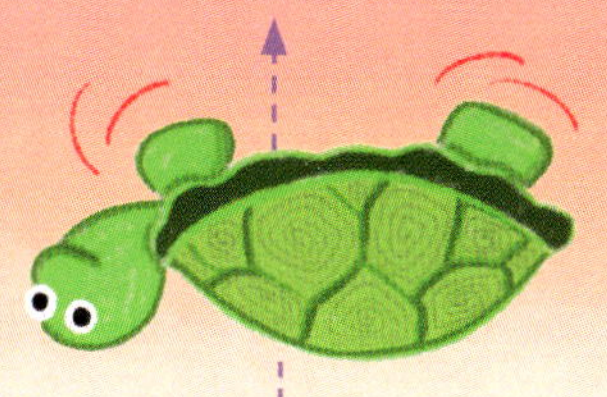

Out of Control

- Feeling super angry
- Feeling super worried
- Feeling overwhelmed
- Feeling panicked
- Feeling super hyper

In the Zone

- Feeling present
- Feeling grounded
- Feeling flexible

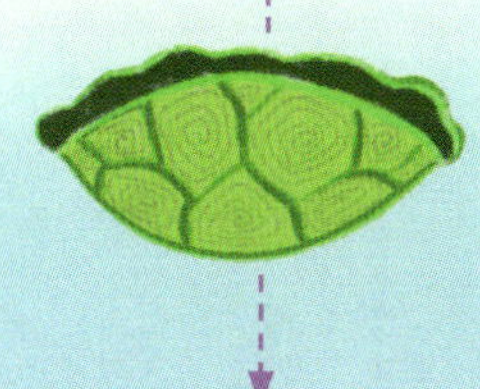

Shut Down

- Hiding away and avoiding
- Feeling low energy
- Feeling super sad
- Feeling numb

Affirmations help us connect to the magic that lives within each of us and remind us of all that we are capable of. Examples include:

I am enough!

I am brave!

I am strong!

I am amazing!

I am loved!

I am capable!

What affirmation are you most excited about today? Take a few moments and recite it out loud or softly to yourself. You might gently rest your palms over your heart and repeat it as many times as you would like.

I am brave
I am loved
I am enough

A Is for Anchors of Attention

An anchor of attention is anything that helps you feel grounded or connected when your thoughts are moving super fast or when you feel overwhelmed. Let's try it together!

From a seated position, look around you to find something that anchors your mind. This could be feeling the sun on your face, watching a butterfly, or simply noticing what you are sitting on. Take note of anything that brings you a sense of connectedness, joy, or ease. Stay there for as long as feels comfortable for you.

B *Is for* Butterfly Hug

The butterfly hug is a practice that can support you when you are having a difficult moment and want to calm down and reconnect to yourself. It's also helpful when you want to provide yourself with love, care, and compassion.

If you'd like, cross your arms across your chest, rest the right side of your cheek on your left palm, and offer yourself a gentle hug. Feel free to explore a gentle rocking motion side to side. Switch sides whenever you feel ready. You are worthy of taking in your own love!

B Is for Breath

Your breath is a powerful tool that you can turn to any time you need to calm or quiet yourself, to release frustration, or to take a moment to slow down.

When you are ready, I invite you to take a deep breath in, and on the exhale, imagine that you are blowing out candles on a cake. Explore this for a couple of breaths, then gently check in with yourself and perhaps relax your shoulders back and down. Notice how you feel and if anything has changed. Your breath is always available to support you!

HAPPY
BIRTHDAY

C *Is for* Community

A community is a supportive group of people who regularly get together and who share common interests! Being part of a community helps us thrive in all areas of our lives. We might find community when we are at school, playing on a sports team, being of service to others, supporting a cause we are passionate about, or spending quality time with friends!

What are some of your favorite ways to be in community with others? How does being with others make you feel? How can you create more community in your life?

ADVENTURE

C *Is for* Creativity

Creativity is a way to express yourself, to find out more about your hobbies and passions, and to practice taking care of yourself. Your creativity is your superpower!

You can practice being creative in everyday moments, whether you are building something with your toys, drawing or making art at school, or using your imagination to share stories that make your eyes sparkle with joy.

What are the ways you like to be creative? How can you carve out time to express your creativity this week?

D *Is for* Dreams

Do you ever daydream about the things you are passionate about? Maybe you dream about traveling the world, growing up to be a veterinarian, or having many loving relationships in your life! Whatever your dreams are, believing in yourself and your dreams is a powerful, everyday practice.

Perhaps take a few moments to write down your dreams or share them with someone you trust. Your dreams are within reach—no matter how big or small. Remind yourself each day that you are worthy and capable of anything you set your mind to.

D *Is for* Delight

When you delight in something, it means that you thoroughly enjoy it and allow yourself to get lost in the experience. This might happen when you are eating your favorite food, doing an activity that brings you so much happiness, or laughing with people you love!

What are some things you find delight in? See if you can take some time to pay attention to that delight as it is happening. This can be a beautiful way to let the joy of the experience ripple throughout the rest of your day!

E *Is for* Empowerment

Empowerment is about making choices that feel best for you! When you are empowered, you honor your own voice, speak up for yourself, and remind yourself that your needs matter. You can also empower others by validating their feelings, supporting them when they feel unsure about something, or simply being a safe space to listen.

Can you reflect back on a time when you felt empowered or empowered others in your life? How did it make you feel? It is truly amazing all that you are capable of!

E *Is for* Ease

When you experience ease, you feel peaceful, happy, and comfortable in your mind and body! We all deserve to experience moments of ease—however that looks for us—whether we're taking a moment to unwind after school, spending time in nature, mindfully coloring or doodling, enjoying a quiet corner in your home, or cuddling with a pet.

What does ease look like for you? What brings you a sense of calm or helps you feel relaxed?

F *Is for* Fun

Did you know that fun, joy, and play help your brain learn and grow?

When you do different fun activities—whether that is visiting a science museum, playing hide-and-seek, working on a puzzle, riding a bike, blowing bubbles, or making friendship bracelets—it helps you explore your world, grow new skills, and take care of your mind and body.

How can you infuse more fun into your days? You deserve it!

F *Is for* Fulfilled

Fulfillment is about feeling content, happy, and satisfied. You might feel fulfilled when you accomplish a challenging goal or task, when you practice kindness by helping a classmate, when you proudly share artwork you have created, when you write your very first sentence or read your first book, or when you complete a season of your favorite team sport.

Can you think of a time when you felt fulfilled? What was that experience like for you? You might take a moment to journal about your experience or discuss it with someone who is special to you!

G *Is for* Grounding

Grounding is a practice that supports you when you are feeling overwhelmed and need a moment to calm yourself. The next time you are feeling stressed or anxious, try grounding yourself with practices like:

- Identifying 5 things you can see, 4 things you can hear, 3 things you can feel, 2 things you can taste, and 1 thing you can smell
- Playing with a fidget toy, pipe cleaner, or modeling clay
- Drinking cold water or splashing cool water on your face
- Taking slow, deep belly breaths at your own pace
- Giving yourself a hug

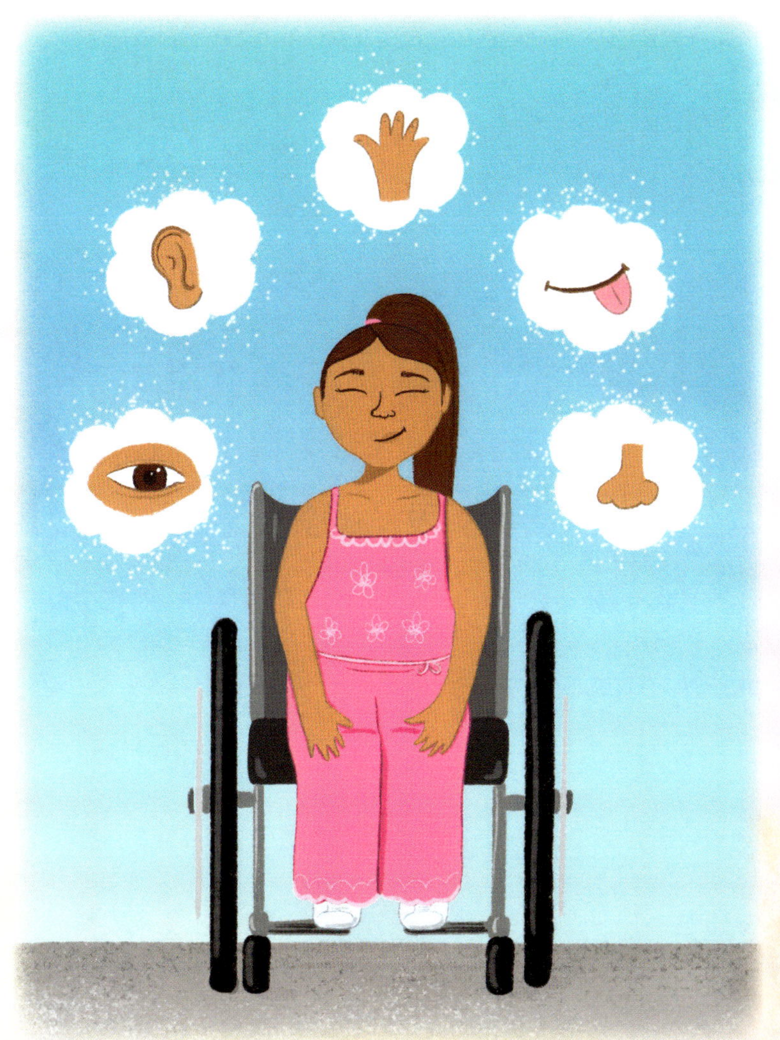

G Is for Gratitude

Gratitude is about being thankful. When you express gratitude to others, it lets them know that they are seen and valued for all they do. You can express gratitude by saying thank you, giving a hug, writing a note, or letting someone know how much they mean to you.

Think about all the people in your life you appreciate, including your friends, family members, coaches, and teachers. You can take time this week to express your gratitude by saying something as simple as "I appreciate you." The impact of your words is truly felt!

H *Is for* Healing

Healing is about being gentle with yourself and taking care of your body and mind when life feels hard. This can be a lifelong process as you face various challenges in life. You might feel sad one day and happy the next, making it sometimes feel like you're on a roller coaster.

But know that you are incredibly resilient, meaning you can bounce back from tough times. You are also deeply supported and never alone in what you're going through.

Take a moment to write down safe people in your life who can support you in your healing. And remember to be kind to yourself.

Be brave

H *Is for* Happiness

Happiness is such a special experience where you feel amused, satisfied, proud, or joyful about something! When you experience happiness, you might feel the warmth of a smile on your face, express yourself with laughter, or feel a sense of contentment inside your body.

What are some things in your life that bring you happiness? These can be little things like going out for ice cream, or big things like feeling proud of your work at school—anything that makes you feel good.

I'm a
star!

I *Is for* Intention

Today, I invite you to explore setting an intention for the day. An intention might be a word you carry with you for inspiration, guidance, and support. You are welcome to choose from these examples or brainstorm your own:

- Energy
- Kindness
- Peace
- Play
- Rest
- Self-compassion
- Strength
- Quiet
- Quality time
- Wonder

If you'd like, you can even write your intention on a stone so you have a physical reminder of your special word!

Wonder

Energy

Kindness

Peace

Strength

Play

Quiet

I *Is for* Inner Strength

You hold so much magic, goodness, and courage within you. These qualities all represent your inner strength, which can be a guiding force in challenging or hard times. It is always there to remind you of all that you are capable of.

When you are ready, I invite you to take a moment to rub your palms together to create a little bit of warmth. Then rest your palms over your heart, taking a moment to reflect on how amazing and strong you are. You are so loved and supported.

J *Is for* Joy

Your joy is beautiful to witness! In the busyness of school and activities, it can be easy to forget to make time for joy. I invite you to take time today to celebrate that deepest part of yourself. Whether it is having a dance party, riding your bike, reading in a special corner of your room, playing with friends at the park, laughing out loud, splashing in the bath, or baking with your family, may you always connect to what brings you joy.

What does joy look like for you, and how can you connect to it today?

J Is for Journey

Life is a journey filled with many ups and downs. On any given day, your nervous system—which works to keep your body in balance—can experience things that bring you joy or sadness, ease or nervousness, calm or overwhelm. This is completely normal, and embracing these various ups and downs will help you build your resilience muscles!

What are some of the highs and lows you've experienced in life? Sending you so much love and care as you embrace your unique journey.

Ease Forest

Waves of
Sadness

Mountains
of Joy

Sea of
Calm

Valley of
Overwhelm

K *Is for* Kindness

Kindness is one of the most important qualities you can have in this big world! Daily acts of kindness can completely change someone's day for the better and inspire even more good deeds. Acts of kindness can include:

- Writing a sweet note
- Holding the door open for someone
- Offering a compliment or sharing your appreciation
- Picking up trash off the floor
- Offering your help

What are some ways you can spread kindness?

K *Is for* Knowing

There are some things only *you* have a deep knowing or intuition about. You may have heard the phrase "trust your gut!" This refers to the way your body "talks" to you about how you feel about something. You can always pay attention to that inner knowing, especially when it comes to what makes you feel comfortable or uncomfortable.

The next time you're not sure about a situation, pay close attention to what your body is telling you, and know that there are always safe adults you can speak to about what you're holding in your mind, body, or heart.

L *Is for* Love

There are so many ways to give and receive love. You can spend quality time with someone, make them a drawing to express how you feel, share snuggles or hold hands if that is comfortable, or tell them something like:

- "I appreciate everything you do for me."
- "I am grateful to have you in my life."
- "You make me feel special."
- "I enjoy being with you."
- "You are so wonderful."

What are some ways you show love? Know that you, too, deserve to be reminded every day that you are loved beyond measure!

L *Is for* Laugh

There is an old saying that "laughter is the best medicine!" Do you ever want to capture those moments when you laugh so hard that your belly and face hurt? Remembering these moments of joy can lift you up when you experience challenges in life.

Think of the last time you could not stop laughing. Maybe you were watching a funny show, telling a joke, chasing a friend at the park, or riding a swing. May you always celebrate those moments of laughter. They are so good for your mind, body, and spirit.

M Is for Mindful

Mindfulness is about slowing down and focusing on whatever is going on in that moment. When you're mindful, you're better able to handle whatever life throws your way.

You can practice mindfulness right now by placing one palm on your belly and one on your heart, focusing your attention on your breath and noticing each time you inhale and exhale. This small but powerful practice can help you pause and settle your nervous system.

Can you think of moments throughout the day when you can benefit from being mindful? Maybe when you wake up in the morning or before playing in a sports game!

M *Is for* Meaning

Finding meaning is about discovering something that is deeply important to you, that you feel passionate about, that excites you, or that gives you a sparkly feeling of goodness inside. You can find meaning in all sorts of different things, including being of service to the community, taking care of a pet, or spending special time with a grandparent!

Meaning can take many different forms—that is what makes it so special and unique! What is something that is meaningful to you?

N *Is for* Nervous System

Your nervous system is made up of a bunch of nerves that run throughout your body and that use physical sensations to let you know how you're feeling. For example, have you ever experienced a tummyache when you feel nervous? Or butterflies when you feel excited? That is your nervous system communicating to you about the different emotions you are feeling!

This week, try taking note of the different ways your nervous system communicates to you, and journal about your experience or talk about it with someone you love.

N *Is for* Nature

Being in nature is one of the most beautiful ways to practice mindfulness, settle your nervous system, and reset your day. Whether you live near the mountains or the ocean, enjoy hikes or neighborhood walks, prefer collecting leaves or listening to the sounds of the birds, the benefits of nature are endless and available just about everywhere!

What is one thing you can do this week to enjoy being in nature?

O Is for Open Heart

When you have an open heart, you're kind, accepting, and generous—and this feeling of goodness inside ripples out to the world.

You might begin your day with this little practice to create a feeling of openheartedness:

> *Take a moment to check in with your heart,*
> *choosing how you'd like to start.*
>
> *Take note of the light that resides deeply within, or close your eyes and simply notice your grin!*
>
> *Your warmth and kindness are a gift*
> *to those you meet.*
>
> *Your presence in the world is so very sweet!*

How can you tend to your open heart today?

O *Is for* Oasis Moment

An oasis is any space (real or imagined!) that gives you a sense of peace, ease, and well-being. Your oasis might be a peaceful place you've been to before or one that you daydream about. You can use your imagination to go anywhere you dream!

You can also create an oasis by surrounding yourself with items that bring you peace or playing sounds of ocean waves to help calm your body and mind.

What does your oasis look like, and when might it be helpful to have an oasis moment during the day?

P *Is for* Peaceful Moment

Feeling at peace is about experiencing a sense of calm, joy, and contentment. You might create peace by taking a few moments in bed at the beginning of the day to take deep breaths in and out at your pace. You might rest a palm on your heart and belly to feel the rise and fall of each breath. As your day unfolds, you can return to this calm place anytime you need a moment to pause and slow down.

When you think about things that bring you peace, what comes to mind?

P *Is for* Patience

Patience is about being able to wait for something you really want or are excited about, whether it's your birthday, a holiday, a toy, a snack, or a trip somewhere. Being patient can be tricky and sometimes make you feel uncomfortable or restless. Some ways to practice patience might be:

- Focusing on your breathing
- Talking about your feelings
- Distracting yourself with another activity you enjoy
- Counting down to your special celebration, toy, treat, or outing

The more you flex your patience muscles, the easier it will become over time!

JUNE
my birthday

Q *Is for* Quiet Time

At the end of a long day, it's important to have a way to wind down that feels gentle, peaceful, and nourishing to you. Consider picking out your comfiest pajamas and creating a quieting ritual with your family. Some ideas might include:

- Listening to comforting music or a podcast sleep story
- Reading a book
- Snuggling with stuffed animals
- Stretching your body
- Taking deep breaths

What would you include in your quiet time?

Q *Is for* Quality Time

One of the sweetest ways you can feel seen and loved is to spend quality time with the people you care about. You can enjoy quality time with someone by playing a board game together, going out to the movies, or holding hands and walking to the park! The important thing is that you simply enjoy each other's company.

What are your favorite ways to spend quality time with the special people in your life? Share your answers with your special people—you can even make a plan to spend time together this week.

R *Is for* Resourcing

Resourcing is the act of identifying a person, place, sound, or item that brings you a feeling of peace, comfort, joy, or calm. You can practice resourcing by:

- Cuddling with a pet or stuffed animal
- Looking out the window to notice the sun in the sky and the breeze in the trees
- Daydreaming about a special place that brings you happiness

As you look around your space, what resources can you identify? The next time you feel tired, overwhelmed, or grumpy, try connecting with this resource and see if your feelings change.

Coloring Book

R *Is for* Rest and Relax

Rest and relaxation are so important to well-being, but it can be hard to slow down in our busy lives. When you need a reminder to slow down, read these words:

> *Take all the time your heart needs.*
>
> *There's no pressure to move with quickness or speed.*
>
> *Be gentle with yourself and honor your pace.*
>
> *Know that everything doesn't need to be a race!*

Then ask yourself how you can quiet your mind and body throughout the day. Perhaps it's resting your head on your desk after recess or laying in the grass and staring up at the clouds!

S Is for Safe

When you feel safe, you feel comforted, supported, and seen. You might feel safe in certain places that bring you a sense of joy and belonging, or when you're around people you trust. No matter what, feeling safe is your greatest right. You deserve to feel safe.

I invite you to take a moment to reflect on who or what helps you feel safe. What are the safe places and people in your life? You might also discuss the word *safety* with your loved ones and explore what this means for you.

S *Is for* Self-Compassion

Self-compassion is about treating yourself with love and care when things feel hard. You can try this self-compassion practice by giving yourself soft squeezes of tenderness:

1. Sit down and bring both palms to the top of your head.
2. Inhale and bring your right palm over your forehead.
3. Exhale and bring your left palm over your heart.
4. On your next inhale, bring your right palm to your belly, then exhale as you rest your left palm over your right—bringing both palms to your belly.

Repeat as many times as you'd like, moving at your own pace.

1
2
3
4
5

T *Is for* Thoughtful

When you're thoughtful, you think about others and show that you care through your words and actions. You can be thoughtful by:

- Giving a friend a tissue when they are crying
- Picking a flower for a loved one
- Making a special drawing for someone
- Helping your family cook a meal
- Opening the door for the person behind you
- Inviting a friend to play
- Sharing your appreciation

What are some thoughtful acts you can do this week?

T *Is for* Tenderness

Tenderness is about showing kindness, love, and gentleness toward yourself and others. You can find tenderness in those sweet moments when you help a friend who has just fallen off their bike, care for yourself as you work through big feelings, or just share a magical moment of connection in the presence of someone you care about.

How can you infuse more tenderness in your day toward yourself and others? You deserve so many tender moments in your life!

U Is for Understanding

Being understanding is about being accepting, compassionate, and open-minded when certain situations don't go as planned. For example, if a friend has to cancel a playdate because they're sick, you can let your friend know that you "get" why they can't come over.

Know that even if you are understanding, it is okay to also feel disappointed. You are absolutely worthy of feeling many different things at the same time!

What are some situations where you've shown understanding to another person? What are some situations where you can practice being more understanding?

U *Is for* Unique and Unapologetically You

You know what is absolutely amazing? YOU! There is no one like you in the whole world, and that is what makes you so very unique and special. You can be anyone you want to be, which means being unapologetically you!

When you think about the different things you love—your hobbies, your passions, or simply what makes you, *you*—what comes to mind? Today, take some time to celebrate these gifts. Self-love and self-celebration are beautiful things!

V Is for Validated

When you feel validated, you feel seen and heard. You feel loved and accepted, just as you are, even when you are experiencing big feelings.

You can also validate others by acknowledging their feelings, expressing your care and concern, or asking them if you can give them a hug. By spreading this type of support and kindness to others, it creates a ripple effect of goodness in the world.

Can you think of a time when someone validated your feelings? How did that make your heart feel?

V Is for Vulnerability

Vulnerability is about opening yourself to others and letting them into your world. This takes courage because when you're vulnerable, you show up in the world *just as you are* without hiding any parts of yourself. It's easier to be vulnerable with people who make you feel safe and like you belong, because you know your feelings will be protected.

Whom in your life can you be vulnerable with? These are people who, no matter what you are feeling or carrying within you, will show you love and care.

W Is for Well-Being

If there is one thing I hope you always carry with you, it is the importance of putting your well-being above all else. You can take care of your overall health and happiness by:

- Moving your body every day
- Reading for fun
- Carving out time for rest, relaxation, and quiet time
- Spending time in nature
- Drinking lots of water
- Spending quality time with friends
- Asking to sit out of an activity that you do not want to do

What are some simple ways you can take care of your body and mind each day?

W *Is for* Wonder

Wonder is about making time for those "wow" moments in life—those moments that amaze you, surprise you, or inspire you. This might be feeling the magic of a ladybug landing on your finger, jumping in rain puddles, or making a fort in your bedroom.

When you seek wonder, you allow your excitement, imagination, joy, and curiosity to guide you. You also take your time instead of feeling rushed by the busyness of life.

What are some ways you like to find wonder in your day? How can you bring more of those "wow" moments into your life?

X *Is for* XOXO

XOXO is an expression that refers to hugs and kisses! It's a way of showing and receiving love, care, and affection.

What are different ways you like to express your affection to others? Whether it is through a hug and a kiss, a high five, a written note, kind words, or anything else that feels comfortable to you and the other person, these feelings of love and connectedness are priceless!

X *Is for* X-Ray

Similar to a real X-ray machine, this practice allows you to look inside your body, see what it's trying to tell you, and honor what it needs.

I invite you to close your eyes and breathe as you focus your attention to different parts of your body, starting with the top of your head and moving down to your shoulders, heart, arms, belly, legs, and feet.

As you scan each area, notice if you feel ease or tension, and respond in a way that feels kind and compassionate. Perhaps that is allowing your body to rest or moving it in a way that feels fun.

Y *Is for* Yoga

Yoga is the Sanskrit word for *union*, which describes the connection between your mind, body, and breath. There are so many incredible yoga shapes that can help you feel calm, strong, confident, balanced, energized, or at ease.

Today, I invite you to try tree pose by imagining you are a tree with roots growing into the ground. If you'd like, begin to balance on your right foot by lifting your left foot up and resting it on your calf or inner thigh. You can put your hand on the wall for extra support or reach your arms up toward the sky like tall branches!

Y *Is for* Yin and Yang

Yin and yang refer to the various opposites in life, like up and down, sun and moon, or movement and rest. You can find balance and well-being in life by using yin and yang as a guide!

For example, if you had a very busy summer day playing outside in the sun, you will want to balance this by drinking lots of water and resting your body. This allows you to care for your nervous system with love and kindness.

Can you think of ways you can balance the yin and yang in your life?

Chips

Z Is for Zen

Zen is a relaxed state of being in the world in which you feel a peaceful and calm energy. To develop this state of being, you might look back to practices in this deck that contain words like *breath*, *ease*, *mindful*, *resourcing*, *grounding*, and *peace*.

After you explore these various practices, see if anything changes in your body and mind. Do you notice greater feelings of relaxation? You might even notice a ripple effect of positive energy that extends to others around you.

Shine
Bright

Z Is for Zigzag

As you go throughout your day, you might encounter several stressful or challenging situations that make you feel a little hyper or even anxious. When this happens, it can be nice to move your body in a zigzag pattern, going from left to right!

Take some time today to explore moving your body, whether you're dancing in the shape of a zigzag, rocking side to side, scribbling back and forth on a piece of paper, marching your feet in place, moving your hips in a hula hoop, practicing fun yoga shapes, or running around in circles. Notice how you feel after!

About the Author

Zabie Yamasaki, MEd, RYT (she/her) is a trauma-informed yoga instructor and trainer, resilience and well-being educator, and sought-after consultant and keynote speaker. Her organization, Transcending Sexual Trauma through Yoga, offers trauma-informed yoga to survivors, consultation for universities and trauma agencies, and training for healing professionals. Zabie has trained thousands of yoga instructors and mental health professionals, and her holistic curriculum is now being implemented at over 40 college campuses. Her work has been highlighted on CNN, NBC, KTLA 5, and The Huffington Post. She is also the author of the *Trauma-Informed Yoga for Survivors of Sexual Assault: Practices for Healing and Teaching with Compassion* book and card deck and *Your Joy Is Beautiful: The Magic of Remembering That You Are Enough, Just As You Are*. She lives in Los Angeles with her beloved partner, son, and their dog, Jack.

www.zabieyamasaki.com

@transcending_trauma_with_yoga

About the Illustrator

Eve Andry (they/she) is a Xicana artist and facilitator. They deeply believe in creativity as a powerful way to tell stories. They have shared their love of art-making with their community for over ten years. In their workshops, Eve compassionately guides participants to use the language of art to express themselves authentically. They love to use color and light as a way to inspire, connect, and heal.

www.eveandry.com
@embody.create.heal

Illustrations by Evelyn Rosario Andry
Cover and interior design by Emily Dyer

ISBN: 9781683737377 (print)
ISBN: 9781683737391 (ePDF)
ISBN: 9781683737384 (KPF)

Printed in the United States of America.

H Is for Healing is a soothing and powerful social-emotional learning (SEL) card deck that provides children with the language for mindfulness, self-compassion, and empowerment. Each card corresponds with a letter of the alphabet and introduces children to an affirmation or activity that will allow them to:

- Regulate their nervous system and find a sense of calm in the world
- Connect to themselves and those around them
- Uncover their delight, joy, and wonder

Together, we can teach our children that they are enough, they are loved, and they belong.